Fact Finders®

WORLD
EXPLORERS

WITHDRAWN

HERNANDO
DE SOTO

An Explorer of the Southeast

by Amie Hazleton

CAPSTONE PRESS
a capstone imprint

Fact Finders Books are published by Capstone Press,
1710 Roe Crest Drive, North Mankato, Minnesota 56003
www.mycapstone.com

Library of Congress Cataloging-in-Publication Data
Names: Hazelton, Amie, author.
Title: Hernando de Soto : an explorer of the Southeast / by Amie Hazelton.
Description: North Mankato, Minnesota : Capstone Press, [2016] | Series: Fact
    finders. World explorers | Includes bibliographical references and index. |
    Audience: Grades 4–6.
Identifiers: LCCN 2016025968 | ISBN 9781515742043 (library binding) | ISBN
    9781515742081 (paperback) | ISBN 9781515742487 (eBook PDF)
Subjects: LCSH: Soto, Hernando de, approximately 1500–1542—Juvenile literature.
    | Explorers—America—Biography—Juvenile literature. | Explorers—Spain—
    Biography—Juvenile literature. | America—Discovery and exploration—
    Spanish—Juvenile literature. | Southern States—Discovery and exploration—
    Spanish—Juvenile literature.
Classification: LCC E125.S7 H39 2016 | DDC 910.92 [B]—dc23
LC record available at https://lccn.loc.gov/2016025968

Editorial Credits:
Alesha Sullivan, editor; Kayla Rossow, designer; Wanda Winch, media researcher;
Laura Manthe, production specialist

Photo Credits:
Bridgeman Images: © Look and Learn/Private Collection/James Edwin McConnell,
16, Index/Museo de America, Madrid, Spain, 9, Photo © Tarker, 13; Capstone, 5;
Granger, NYC - All rights reserved, 7; North Wind Picture Archives, cover inset,
11, 19, 20, 27; Science Source: Robin Treadwell, 23; Shutterstock: arigato, cardboard
texture, Ensuper, scratch paper texture, Nik Merkulov, grunge paper element, run4it,
watercolor paper element, Sunny Forest, sky design element, William Silver, cover
background

Printed in China.
009943S17

TABLE OF CONTENTS

Growing Up with a Dream

Hernando de Soto was born in 1500 in Jérez de los Caballeros, Spain. His parents were **nobles**, born in nearby Badajoz. Besides Hernando and Juan, the couple had two daughters, Catalina and Maria. They lived in Jérez de los Caballeros, a bustling market town lined with houses and shops. Even as a boy, Hernando de Soto knew he would leave his southwestern Spanish home someday.

When his parents died, Hernando's older brother, Juan, would inherit everything they owned. That was the law in Spain. Younger sons, like Hernando, would get nothing.

FACT!

In the 1500s southwestern Spain was harsh and rocky. It was covered in dry, dusty fields. But there was something special about this part of Spain. It produced some of Spain's greatest explorers—Francisco Pizarro, Vasco Núñez, and Hernán Cortés.

noble—aristocratic; belonging to a class with high social or political status

Even as a boy, Hernando had big dreams. Hernando could never have imagined what his future really held, however. He would grow up to fight his way through the Americas. He would become wealthier than he ever dreamed. And he would stumble upon a mighty river—bigger than any river in Europe.

De Soto's Journeys

The Early Years

Jérez de los Caballeros was surrounded by high stone walls to keep out wild animals and robbers. The **Moors** had invaded Spain in AD 711. The Moor government was wealthy and powerful. The Spaniards eventually drove out the Moors. With the Moors' defeat in 1492, Spain was at peace for the first time in more than 800 years. Now young men such as de Soto had to look elsewhere for adventure.

The year 1492 brought another important event—Christopher Columbus sailed west across the Atlantic Ocean from Spain. Columbus hoped to discover the Indies. The Indies were a group of Asian islands abundant with spices, pearls, silk, and other treasures. Columbus never got to the Indies. Instead, he sailed the wrong way and came upon a whole new world—the Americas.

Moor—a member of the Arab peoples who practices the religion of Islam

conquistador—a leader in the Spanish conquest of the Americas

An engraving depicts the departure of a Spanish voyage to the New World in the 1500s.

Columbus thought he had found the Indies, so he called the people who lived there "Indians." After hearing of possible riches in the Americas, several Spanish ships set sail westward. Their leaders were known as **conquistadors**. These men conquered most of South America, Central America, and Mexico. The priests who traveled with the conquistadors hoped to convert the native peoples to Christianity. But the conquistadors believed the Americas held gold and glory.

Chapter 1

HEADED TO THE AMERICAS

When Hernando was 14 years old, his father sent him to the busy harbor city of Seville, Spain. Seville was the largest city Hernando had ever seen. On the banks of the Guadalquivir River, men were loading ships with tools, weapons, and food. Hernando was to sail west with a man named Pedro Árias Dávila, also known as Pedrarias. Hernando was afraid of Pedrarias because he was known to be very strict and cruel to those who worked for him. But Pedrarias was one of King Ferdinand II's most trusted leaders.

Pedrarias welcomed Hernando and immediately put him to work on the ship. They were loading up to set sail for the **colony** of Darién, which is the present-day nation of Panama in Central America. Pedrarias was set to be the new governor there.

At dawn on April 11, 1514, a **fleet** of 20 ships left Seville carrying more than 2,000 people. Hernando could hear trumpets playing a farewell from the shore. At last the ships sailed through the Guadalquivir's mouth and into the massive Atlantic Ocean. From there they would sail across the sea. It would be 22 years before Hernando saw Spain again.

colony—a territory settled by people from another country and controlled by that country
fleet—a number of ships that form a group

Hernando must have felt proud of participating in Pedrarias's journey. Everyone in his hometown had heard of Darién. The man who started the colony, Vasco Núñez Balboa, had also grown up in Jérez de los Caballeros. One year earlier, Balboa journeyed across the **Isthmus** of Panama, the narrow strip of land separating the Atlantic and Pacific oceans. Balboa was the first European to set eyes on the Pacific.

VASCO NÚÑEZ BALBOA

During Balboa's journey through the Isthmus of Panama, native peoples told him that a province rich in gold was located to the south. But the natives said the Spaniards would need at least 1,000 men to conquer those lands. Balboa refused to request more men from Spain. The possibility of finding gold created excitement. A large expedition was quickly planned. But Balboa was not given command of the trip. Instead King Ferdinand II sent the elderly Pedrarias to lead the voyage.

isthmus—a narrow strip of land that connects two larger areas of land and lies between two bodies of water

After nearly two months of sailing, the fleet stopped at the Caribbean island of Dominica. This is where Hernando learned how cruel Pedrarias could be. While some ships were being repaired, a number of sailors wandered off and got drunk. When it was time to leave, one man refused to board the ship, so Pedrarias had him hanged. Hernando quickly learned that Pedrarias was a man to be obeyed.

Balboa claimed the Pacific Ocean for Spain in 1513.

At last the ships sailed into a bay at Darién. Balboa was running the colony fairly and peacefully. The native peoples welcomed Balboa wherever he went and presented him with many gifts. Hernando admired Balboa, and the two became friends.

But Pedrarias wrecked the peace that Balboa had established with the native peoples. Pedrarias's men stormed through one native village after another. The men stole what they could and killed any American Indian who stood in their way. Pedrarias was fond of Hernando and sent him on many missions. Hernando witnessed the Spaniards' raids and how Pedrarias and his men killed natives. The native people had little defense against the Spaniards' guns and swords.

FACT!

Hernando de Soto ran a gold mine in Nicaragua and was involved in the Indian slave trade. About 650,000 Indians in Nicaragua, Honduras, and Costa Rica were enslaved in the 1500s.

Hernando de Soto

By 1521 Hernando had earned the title of Captain de Soto. Three years later at the age of 24, the young captain took part in the **conquest** of Nicaragua. Next he explored El Salvador and Honduras. The following year, Pedrarias put de Soto in command of an army in Nicaragua.

As a reward for his services, Hernando was given a large piece of land. Along with the land, Hernando was allowed to use local American Indians as his slaves. By this time, de Soto was wealthy and living comfortably. Yet he wanted more.

conquest—something that is taken over, such as land, treasure, or buildings

Chapter 2
THE DEFEAT OF PERU

Everyone from Spain knew of Hernán Cortés, the man who had stolen the riches from the Aztecs in Mexico. Now rumors circulated that the Incas in Peru also had gold. And de Soto knew the man who planned to find the Peruvian gold—Francisco Pizarro.

Francisco Pizarro was a soldier in Darién. Now he wanted to head south to the Inca **Empire**. Stretching down South America's western coastline, the Inca Empire was five times the size of Spain. Inca **craftsmen** carved huge stones and fit them perfectly together to form buildings and other large structures. Gold, silver, and copper were dug out of Inca mines. But the Spaniards cared only about the gold.

In 1530 Pizarro asked de Soto to join him on the conquest of the Incas, but de Soto was afraid of Pizarro. Pedrarias ordered Pizarro and his crew not to go because he wanted to be the one claiming the riches from the Inca. Without permission, Pizarro was forced to hold off on venturing to Peru. However, in 1531 Pedrarias died, and Pizarro no longer had any reason to wait to take his trip.

INCA ROAD SYSTEM

The Incas had an incredible system of roads, stretching over 14,000 miles (22,531 km). The roads and bridges were the result of good engineering and skill. The road system ran through valleys and over mountains. In some areas the roads were smooth and paved, carefully laid out with stones. Bridges were the only way to cross over rivers by foot. If a bridge suffered damage, the locals would repair it as quickly as possible. All across the Inca Empire, roads and bridges were swept clean. Lodging and temples to the sun were located along many roads for travelers.

empire—a group of countries that have the same ruler

craftsperson—someone who is skilled at making things with his or her hands

While on the voyage to Peru, de Soto was in charge of Pizarro's **horsemen**. From the coast, the men marched up the rocky foothills of the Andes Mountains in Peru. The Spaniards were heading for the city of Cajamarca. There they would meet the Inca **emperor** Atahualpa, who was also known as the Sun King.

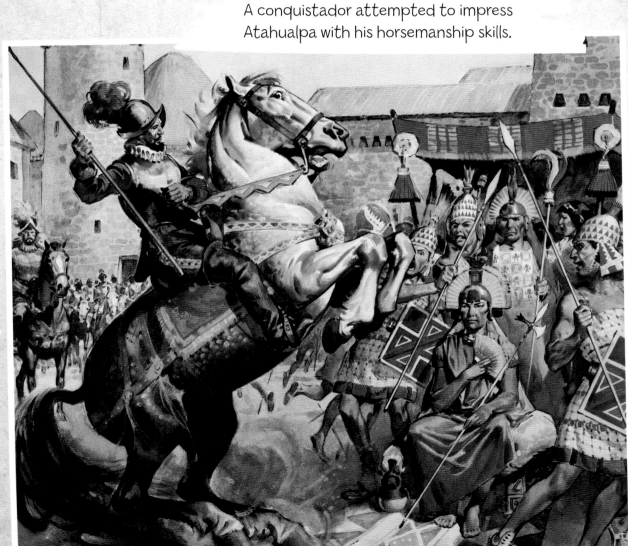

A conquistador attempted to impress Atahualpa with his horsemanship skills.

On the way to Cajamarca, de Soto and his men passed through Cajas. The chief in Cajas treated them well and gave them food. But de Soto repaid that kindness with cruelty. More than 500 religious women lived in the city's Temple of the Sun. De Soto forced the women outside and divided the women up among his men. Angry Inca warriors were prepared to attack, but de Soto's men killed them all.

The Spaniards continued their journey, and at last they came upon the city of Cajamarca. Pizarro sent de Soto to meet the Inca leader there. De Soto would be the first European to meet the Sun King.

Emperor Atahualpa's nobles were dressed in sparkling robes adorned with pearls and gold. Atahualpa sat on a stool wearing a red wool headdress. De Soto delivered a fine speech, but the emperor never looked up. De Soto tried to impress Atahualpa by making his horse prance and twirl in circles. Atahualpa seemed to enjoy the tricks. Finally Atahualpa listed de Soto's crimes. The emperor's spies had told him everything.

horseman—a rider on horseback
emperor—the leader of an empire, which is a group of countries

But Pizarro had a different plan to win the emperor's affection. He invited Atahualpa to dinner. When the emperor arrived, Pizarro demanded that the emperor become a Christian. Atahualpa tossed Pizarro's bible on the ground.

Spanish soldiers rushed out from all sides. All through the night, fighting went on. By morning more than 5,000 Inca were dead. Pizarro took Atahualpa captive. Pizarro promised the Inca that he would free Atahualpa if they brought him riches. Animals carrying loads of gold and silver arrived from all over the empire. Pizarro collected more than 11 tons (9.8 tonnes) of goods from the Inca. Then Pizarro had the emperor killed.

De Soto was furious. De Soto had become friends with Atahualpa and respected him. But de Soto had no choice but to continue to follow orders. He was the first European to enter Cuzco, the Incan capital city. De Soto's job was to conquer. He attacked Cuzco and left with a fortune in gold. In 1535 de Soto sailed back to Spain—a very wealthy man.

Pizarro ordered the execution of Atahualpa after Pizarro collected gold and riches from the Inca.

Chapter 3

DE SOTO'S EMPIRE

Back in Spain, de Soto was treated like a hero. In 1536 he married Pedrarias's daughter, Isabella de Bobadilla. But something was missing for him—Spain was boring compared to life in the Americas. In 1537 King Charles of Spain made de Soto governor of Cuba, a Caribbean island. Upon the king's orders, de Soto was also supposed to go to Florida to set up a colony.

De Soto arrived in Florida in 1539.

De Soto knew conquering Florida would not be easy. Several Spaniards had tried and failed to set up a colony in Florida. Native peoples shot and killed Spanish explorer Juan Ponce de León there in 1521. And when Pánfilo de Narváez tried to take over Florida, only four of his men survived. But de Soto was determined because he had heard Florida was full of gold and riches as great as those of Mexico and Peru. This was de Soto's chance to conquer an empire, just as Cortés and Pizarro had.

FACT!

De Soto and his men brought along horses and dogs, and hundreds of pigs for food.

More than 600 men went to Florida with de Soto. On May 25, 1539, de Soto stepped ashore just south of present-day Tampa Bay, Florida. De Soto and his men traveled deep into the swamps and forests of central Florida. Alligators crept through the swamps, squealing wild boars ran in every direction, and bright pink flamingoes sprinkled the landscape. De Soto had never seen anything like it.

When winter came, de Soto and his men stayed in an Apalachee Indian village called Anhaica, near present-day Tallahassee, Florida. In the spring, they pushed north through what is now Georgia and South Carolina. They entered a kingdom called Cofitachequi, and its chief was a beautiful woman. Her royal city was lined with houses and a grand temple. The queen greeted de Soto warmly and gave him many gifts, including long strings of pearls.

De Soto's crew begged him to settle down and build the colony there. But there was no gold to be found, so de Soto moved on. He took the queen as prisoner so that her village would continue to provide de Soto and his men with food. Later, the queen managed to escape, and de Soto pushed north toward North Carolina and Tennessee.

FACT!

One of the bloodiest battles of the era began shortly after Choctaw chief Tuscaloosa brought de Soto to Mabila. Tuscaloosa even gathered women and children to help drive out de Soto from the Choctaw empire. De Soto won the battle by setting the town on fire. Hundreds of Indians died.

De Soto took another Indian chief as prisoner from the empire of Coosa in northwest Georgia. For three months, de Soto marched through Coosa, demanding slaves and food. Again, his men begged him to stop and build the colony. But de Soto wanted only gold.

The Cofitachequi presented de Soto with pearls and gifts.

This time the Spaniards headed south through Alabama where they met Tuscaloosa, a Choctaw chief. Tuscaloosa invited de Soto into the city of Mabila, near present-day Mobile, Alabama. The Spaniards were looking forward to relaxing. Meanwhile, Tuscaloosa gathered his warriors together to take on de Soto and his men.

Chapter 4
THE LAST ADVENTURE

During the following winter, de Soto marched his men through Mississippi. The supplies and clothing they'd gotten in Cofitachequi were all destroyed in Mabila. Many of de Soto's men were wounded, and others fled. The remaining loyal followers barely survived the snowy, cold winter.

On May 8, 1541, de Soto's men reached the widest river they had ever seen—the Mississippi. It is often said that de Soto discovered the river, but many other explorers had seen the mouth of the river years earlier. De Soto, however, was the first European to encounter the Mississippi by land.

But de Soto wasn't impressed. Instead, he was annoyed by the river's great size. His men spent months building rafts to cross the wide river.

De Soto and his men eventually crossed the Mississippi into Arkansas. Indians there told de Soto stories about gold in a nearby kingdom called Pacaha. De Soto rushed to Pacaha but found no gold. At this point de Soto was not sure what to do. He wandered the foothills of the Ozark Mountains, and his scouts searched west into Oklahoma. But the flat plains did not look promising for a golden empire.

In the fall de Soto turned south toward Louisiana. Many of his men had left him, and the remaining were all weak or sick. By winter de Soto himself was sick with a fever. He knew he was going to die soon. De Soto decided that Luis de Moscoso would take over his mission as leader of the group.

Hernando de Soto died on May 21, 1542, near the banks of the Mississippi River. Moscoso and his men put de Soto's body in a log that was hollowed out, weighed it down, and placed it in the Mississippi, where it sank. Only about 300 Spaniards were left in the group—fewer than half of those who began. Under Moscoso's rule, they wandered through Arkansas, Texas, and Louisiana. Eventually they reached the Mississippi again and floated down to the Gulf of Mexico, sailing to Mexico. People were shocked to see them because they had been gone so long. Everyone thought they were dead.

De Soto's **expedition** failed to establish a colony in Florida. He became too greedy to bother being a good explorer for Spain. But at least one good thing came out of de Soto's explorations. A few men who survived the journey reported everything that they saw. Their reports tell us how Indians lived in the American Southeast before they lost their native lands.

expedition—a long journey for a special purpose, such as exploring
ethnographer—someone who studies the customs of individual peoples and cultures

De Soto's men buried him in the Mississippi River.

WRITTEN ACCOUNTS

Three of de Soto's men wrote narratives about the expedition. The first was Elvas, an unnamed participant in the expedition. The second was Rodrigo Rangel, who was de Soto's private secretary. The third was Luys Hernández de Biedma, the king's representative during the voyage. The men's first-hand accounts of the American Southeast were written when they returned to Spain after de Soto's death. About 50 years later, an **ethnographer** named Garcilaso de la Vega assembled the stories into one book. These stories are the oldest written records of life in North America.

Timeline

711–1492: The Moors invade Spain in AD 711; Spain defeated the Moors in 1492

1492: Italian explorer Christopher Columbus sets sail from Spain across the Atlantic Ocean

1500: Hernando de Soto is born in Jérez de los Caballeros, Spain

1513: Vasco Núñez de Balboa becomes the first European to see the Pacific Ocean

1514: De Soto ventures across the Atlantic Ocean for the first time with Pedro Árias Dávila, also known as Pedrarias

1524: De Soto takes part in the conquest of Nicaragua

1531: Pizarro and de Soto begin the conquest of Peru

1535: De Soto returns to Spain and marries Pedrarias's daughter, Isabella de Bobadilla

1537: King Charles of Spain makes de Soto governor of Cuba; de Soto is also told to set up a colony in Florida

1539: De Soto arrives at Tampa Bay, Florida, and begins exploring the southeastern United States

1541: De Soto reaches the Mississippi River by land

1542: De Soto dies of a fever; his body is wrapped in a hollow log and sinks to the bottom of the Mississippi River

Important People

Vasco Núñez de Balboa (1475–1519)—first European to look upon the Pacific Ocean

Charles I (1500–1558)—king of Spain, and Holy Roman Emperor (as Charles V)

Christopher Columbus (1451–1506)—explorer who reached the Americas in 1492

Hernán Cortés (1485–1547)—conqueror of Mexico's Aztec Empire

Pedro Árias Dávila (Pedrarias) (1440–1531)—Spanish governor of Panama and Nicaragua

Juan Ponce de León (1460?–1521)—first Spanish explorer to reach Florida

Francisco Pizarro (1475?–1541)—conqueror of the Inca Empire in Peru

GLOSSARY

colony (KOL-uh-nee)—a territory settled by people from another country and controlled by that country

conquest (KON-kwest)—something that is taken over, such as land, treasure, or buildings

conquistador (kon-KEYS-tuh-dor)—a leader in the Spanish conquest of the Americas

craftsperson (KRAFTS-per-suhn)—someone who is skilled at making things with his or her hands

emperor (EM-pur-ur)—the leader of an empire, which is a group of countries

empire (EM-pire)—a group of countries that have the same ruler

ethnographer (eth-NOG-ruh-fer)—someone who studies the customs of individual peoples and cultures

expedition (ek-spuh-DISH-uhn)—a long journey for a special purpose, such as exploring

fleet (FLEET)—a number of ships that form a group

horseman (HORSS-min)—a rider on horseback

isthmus (ISS-muhss)—a narrow strip of land that connects two larger areas of land and lies between two bodies of water

Moor (MOOR)—a member of the Arab peoples who practices the religion of Islam

noble (NOH-buhl)—aristocratic; belonging to a class with high social or political status

READ MORE

Conklin, Wendy. *Finding Florida: Exploration and Its Legacy.* Primary Source Readers. Huntington Beach, Calif.: Teacher Created Materials, 2017.

Santella, Andrew. *Southeast Indians. First Nations of North America.* Chicago: Heinemann Library, 2012.

Stuckey, Rachel. *Explore with Hernando de Soto. Travel with the Great Explorer.* New York: Crabtree Publishing, 2016.

INTERNET SITES

FactHound offers a safe, fun way to find Internet sites related to this book. All of the sites on FactHound have been researched by our staff.

Here's all you do:

Visit *www.facthound.com*

Type in this code: 9781515742043

Super-cool stuff! Check out projects, games and lots more at **www.capstonekids.com**

CRITICAL THINKING USING THE COMMON CORE

1. What was Hernando de Soto's goal in launching an expedition back to North America in 1539? Why was this goal so important to the Spanish? (Key Ideas and Details)

2. Why do you think de Soto's men buried him in the Mississippi River? (Integration of Knowledge and Ideas)

3. Why do you think Spanish exploration in the American Southeast had a negative impact on native cultures? (Integration of Knowledge and Ideas)

INDEX